The Angel Corps

The Angel Corps: The Necessity of Putting Others First

Andy Boerger

ISBN-10: 1-91-260531-7
ISBN-13: 978-1-912605-31-6

Published by j-views Publishing, 2018

© 2015, 2018 Andy Boerger and j-views Publishing

All rights reserved. Without limiting the rights under copyright reserved above, no part of this publication may be reproduced, stored in or introduced into a retrieval system, or transmitted, in any form, or by any means (electronic, mechanical, photocopying, recording, or otherwise) without the prior written permission of both the copyright owner and the above publisher of this book.

www.j-views.biz
andysart-andyboerger.blogspot.jp

j-views Publishing, 26 Lombard Street, Lichfield, UK, WS13 6DR
publish@j-views.biz

Contents

Acknowledgments & Sundry iv
Praise for "The Angel Corps" v
Introduction 3
I'm In! 7
The proud, the few 13
What About Those Harps? 19
'Angel Moments' .23
Our Duties to Smaller Ones 41
Try a Little Tenderness 51
Let Your Left Hand Know… 57
Angels, NOT Doormats 63
1% Inspiration, 99% Desperation 69
Words ARE Deeds .73
Angels Everywhere! 77
Conclusion: So, Are You In? 81
About the Author .86

Acknowledgments & Sundry

This being a book about helping and being helped, if I were to undertake to acknowledge, by listing, everyone who has helped me throughout my life, this section would end up much longer than the book itself. Angels have been looking out for me for as long as I can remember, and to each and everyone, I am deeply grateful. You have made this book possible.

Among these, I wish to acknowledge the angelic words and deeds of my mother, Rose; Greg and Don May; Charles Bellows; Rae Chandron; Glynis Wozniak; Betty Buttress, Beth Boerger and Taro Muramatsu.

Special thanks to the 'anonymous angel' who did the layout for this book, and to the Boss of Beans and all the dedicated staff and extended family that is InknBeans Press.

I dedicate this book to all of you, and to M.M.

The book is loosely, and not always precisely, divided into two parts: 'stories' (which appear with a gray background) and 'lessons' (with no background). The stories are drawn from my own life, while the lessons are there to shed light on various features of The Angel Corps that the stories exemplify. The reason for this is simple; this book is not intended to be read as a memoir. It is my hope that reading the stories evokes memories of readers' own, parallel, stories, perhaps inspiring the thought, "why, of course! The Angel Corps! It's been there all along!".

All the artwork that appears in the book was created by me, though the cover and the inner work were created at different periods of my life, and are thus quite different in style. Some readers may wonder, 'what's with the elephants?' I ask them to simply indulge an artist in his peculiarities. I like to draw elephants; that's it.

Praise for "The Angel Corps"

Andy Boerger begins by writing, "This is a self help book about helping others." He declares and abundantly illustrates that "life goes better when we put others first." Jesus gave us the ultimate embodiment of this principle, when he gave up his own life for others while on earth and the cross.

Andy writes that he uses the word "angel" more as a verb than a noun. So that when we help others we are engaging in one of the tasks of God's angels. Yet, even in our surrender to service, we receive the greater reward in our own lives.

He looks at the future of civilization, recognizes constant setbacks, and calls for people to enlist in "The Angel Corps". Andy envisions a world where everyone puts others first, thereby helping to get our society back on track, or "perhaps even allowing it to survive at all."

Dr. Philip Eyster, author of Soaring Higher

The Angel Corps

The Necessity of Putting Others First

Andy Boerger

J-views Publishing, Lichfield, England

*Some days you'll be sailing,
on others be flailing
and still others lost in a funk;
but however it goes
every elephant knows
if you can't lend a hand, lend a trunk!*

Introduction

This is a self help book about helping others. That's less paradoxical than it may appear at first blush. In my half century of life, I've learned - perhaps you have as well - that happiness comes more through being than having. So, the question becomes, what kind of being? When we are being self-focused, we might find happiness, or we might not. That way often leads to continual insecurity. Am I good enough? Are the people around me good enough? Am I getting all I can out of life? Have I accomplished enough? Earned enough? If we imagine that happiness comes as a result of eventually being able to check off 'yes' to each of those questions, then the risk is that we will often find ourselves alone on a field with continually switching goalposts. We may feel that we are walking atop jello to get to where we want to be. Sometimes we are there, sometimes we are not. There is an impermanence that is built into the idea that happiness comes from continually feeding the maw of goals, desires and ambitions.

Mightn't, on the other hand, happiness be something as

simple as liking oneself? Now, probably tomorrow, and most of the time? Is that a reasonable way to think of happiness? That, when I like myself I am happy, just as I am happy when I am around other people I like, books I like, pets I like, food I like, etc? If such is the case, then I can confidently state that simple gestures of kindness toward others is one of the surest ways to be a happy person, since performing them makes us more genuinely likable, to ourselves and to others. Such gestures form a necessary ingredient in happy lives, and are one of the best things to fall back on when our own personal goals and desires are waning rather than waxing.

Thus, there will be no declaration within these pages that the Universe is akin to a genie that you need to learn how to rub the right way, or a secret that, when discovered, leads to every Porsche and luxury cruise your heart desires. My suspicion is that such declarations are better at producing initial highs than they are at sustaining long term happiness. I think that when a book or author jubilantly assures you that 'You can be happy!', the important thing to consider is which 'you' is being addressed? Is it the 'you' that is focused on desires, and the list of questions above? Or is it the deeper 'you' that is much more than desires, yearnings and various metrics of accomplishments and success? Each of us is ever so much more than that.

What you will find in these pages are stories about an extraordinary 'organization' that is in the business of helping people be happy, and has been for a very, very long time. It is an organization you may already be a member of. In any case, it's one that has surely touched your life. It was involved in some of your profoundest experiences. Perhaps, as you read these stories, they will remind you of similar moments in your own life, when you played the role of someone's angel, or someone played that role for you.

There is but one central theme running throughout the stories that follow, and it is simplicity itself: life goes better when we put others first. Joy results. Healing happens. A higher plane of human experience is touched, however briefly. Imagine a million such stories occurring each day. Imagine the ripple effects that are yielded. Such is the way of the Angel Corps. May it become a way of life, and usher in a new chapter, long overdue, in human history.

Let's turn a page, and explore the lifestyle of putting others first.

After you…

I'm In!

When I first noticed the dog, a scruffy terrier, up ahead of me, he was walking at precisely the distance from the elderly Japanese man that one would expect between a dog and his owner. Thus, my mind rushed to the conclusion that they were a pair. The absence of a leash was, however, curious. It is very rare in Tokyo to see dogs being walked untethered. But, I wasn't in Tokyo. I was in a suburb two hours east, on a day-long teaching assignment. Perhaps the relative sparseness of the population in these parts afforded owners - and their dogs - greater leniency. I was spending my lunch hour walking along a pleasant course that ran along what had once been a narrow stream, since dried up, sharing the course with only these two figures -one two-legged, one four-legged - who moved toward me from the opposite direction.

As the dog wandered on further ahead of the man, and then further still, my earlier assumption seemed doubtful. There was no apparent connection between the two; they seemed completely indifferent to one another. Eventually, the dog passed right by me, without looking up. It was by now well ahead of the man, still a good thirty yards back. I noticed he was looking off in another direction, his concern elsewhere. This was plainly odd. There were plenty of stray cats all over the endless expanse of Tokyo and its suburbs, but a dog? I guessed the dog was lost. As my lunch break lasted another forty five minutes, I turned to walk alongside it.

All the while, the dog paid no attention to me. It just kept on walking, purposefully, stopping every once in a while to sniff at something or other. I, on the other hand, paid plenty attention to it. I was trying to learn as much about it as I could. It looked pretty old, and seemed to be fed and cared for. It was wearing a cheap blue plastic collar that, upon further observance, had some numbers written on it in marker. These I recognized as a telephone number. Now, I was getting somewhere.

The problem was that, being unfamiliar with the area, I couldn't telephone the dog's owner even with the number on the collar, because it didn't include the area code. By now, the dog and I had left the walking course and were moving through a small, nearly empty outdoor shopping mall. A young mother was there with her two children. The younger of the two pointed to the dog, and the three of them started chatting about it. The mother would almost certainly know the area code, but stopping to ask her meant perhaps losing sight of the dog. He just kept on walking! He had been on the move constantly, nose to the ground, barely looking up, since I had first seen him. A sniffing missile.

Fortunately, just as I began to, hurriedly, talk to the mother (who naturally had assumed that I was the owner), the old man from the walking course came by. As it turned out, he had also been concerned about the dog, and from a distance had kept an eye on both of us. Perhaps seeing me stop and talk to the mother gave him a bit of courage to speak to me. Japanese can be very shy, and reluctant to engage strangers, particularly those of the older generations such as him. Also, he may have concluded the dog was mine, just as I originally had thought it was his.

Thus, we had a small team of 'angels' assembled. It was a relief to see the mother and the old man share my concern for the dog. It was a boost to know that I would be supported in my mission (chosen barely five minutes earlier) of getting him back where he belonged. The two children, meanwhile, found the whole thing to be an intriguing adventure. Five people can keep an eye on one dog, no matter how set upon his own ways he is. The mother called the number while I followed the dog. The old man maintained more or less equal distance between us to act as a relay. Luckily, the dog's owner picked up the phone right away, confirmed that her dog had strayed that morning, and said she would be on her way. Now it was just a matter of keeping the dog from wandering too far off, while we all waited for her to arrive.

From the owner, the mother learned the dog's name, and got assurances that he wouldn't bite. These, the old man shouted to me. The scene was surely comical, people passing along information about a dog who was in his own world. But without those two vital pieces of information, I really didn't see any choice but to simply follow the ol' fella where he led. I didn't want to get bitten. I've been around dogs all my life and have virtually no fear of them, but I didn't want to return to my workplace with a bloody hand in need of bandaging.

Calling his name, gently tugging on him, etc., I was able to contain him better, and we were all able to converge around a small area and keep a lookout for the owner. She arrived on a bicycle about ten minutes later. After being profusely thanked by the owner, petting the dog, playing a bit with the two kids, and - with the mother and older gentleman - basking in such feelings of relief and camaraderie as are always called for upon the successful completion of a mission, I returned to my job, getting back almost on the dot. Though the episode was unexpected, it was hardly unusual. It was just another in a long line of 'operations' I've participated in since joining the Angel Corps.

The Proud, the Few

Do *you* have what it takes to join the Angel Corps? Why, of course you do! No other organization demands so little of you in return for all the benefits it provides. There is a good chance you already are a member. Some people have always known about the Corps (without referring to it as such) and appear to abide by its principles naturally. Others need to be reminded of its existence, and a bit of encouragement to enlist. They (we, since I count myself among this group) just need that extra tap on the shoulder. Still others need to be taught about it from scratch, perhaps imagining that its protocols are somehow alien to their nature. But, they aren't, and joining the Angel Corps will soon teach them that they aren't. The only things anyone need to change or put aside to join the Corps are things that haven't served them all that well anyway.

There is just one requirement: to become – and remain – a member of the Corps, you agree to put others first. That's it. On an average day, there may arise one, or several, opportunities to be of service to someone. You agree that most of the time (as often as possible) when such moments appear in your life - as they surely will - you will provide the help that the situation calls for. Each morning, when you wake up, you confirm your membership by proclaiming, "I'm in". When you say this, silently or aloud, you acknowledge that life will often present you with situations where your service is called for, perhaps that very day. Furthermore, that you welcome such moments, and commit to your role of helper. Of 'angel'.

A perfect tally isn't required. There will be times when you are perhaps too tired, too preoccupied, or just not in the right frame of mind. You're human. But in such cases (and even as you cut yourself some slack, as you should) you will recognize that an opportunity was missed, and one less act of service was performed on this earth. You recommit to the principles of the Corps, and get back on your horse. Nevertheless, the focus is not upon missed opportunities, but rather taken ones. Most of the time, when you see someone in need, you WILL help. You are a member of the Angel Corps, and service is now your calling. People, animals, the planet, etc., need help. The collective needs of life on earth are great beyond measure. Thus, help is necessary. A member of the Angel Corps recognizes this, and embraces it as an opportunity.

Here are some of the Angel Corps activities I participated in over the last week or so, either through giving, or receiving, help:

- ❈ a petite mother faced the daunting task of carrying a heavy baby buggy up a long flight of stairs at a train station. Confusion changed to relief, and finally to a huge smile on her face, when the task of hoisting and

carrying the buggy up the stairs was accomplished for her
- a passenger on a train platform was obviously about to get on the wrong train, based upon his overheard mobile phone conversation. Being told that he needed to wait for the next train saved him a lot of hassle
- a copy of *The Big Issue* was purchased from a homeless salesman near Shinjuku station. The magazine was handed over along with a handful of gratis candies; thus service was provided from both parties
- a stray cat clearly welcomed the attention as a passerby stopped to pet him, rub his chin, and simply take the time to show him he was loved and valued
- a friend is trying to get a side business going, without much luck so far. She appreciated the purchase of a not particularly wanted item to help her out
- a concert-goer foolishly chose to ignore the forecast of rain, and was umbrella-less when the ending of the concert coincided with a torrential downpour, as forecast. All was not lost, as a kindly member of the auditorium staff produced an old, unclaimed plastic umbrella and said not to worry about returning it
- an unlucky worm had wandered onto a stretch of paved sidewalk and was hopelessly flailing about, until it was picked up along with a small clump of dirt, carried to a moist patch of soil, and placed inside
- the sink in the teacher's break room where I work occasionally fills up with unwashed coffee cups, etc., and it usually falls on the office staffers to wash what the teachers leave behind in a rush to get to their next class. A teacher has made it a habit to wash every cup, saucer, spoon, etc. in the sink, in addition to his own. Some other teachers have gradually taken the cue and begun to do the same thing

❈ a female high school student was unselfconsciously working on some sketches of elephants she had begun during a field trip to the zoo that day. Some words of encouragement from the man seated next to her, himself an artist, caused her to beam as she told of her dreams to study art in New York or Los Angeles. She was nearly floating as she stepped off the train

Clearly, in all cases, the cost to the giver was exceedingly small. There was no burden; all that was required was some acute observation of one's surroundings and a willingness to be of service. In each case, the benefit to the receiver outweighed, in some cases by far, the cost to the giver. Angel Corps operations are like that. They ask very little from us in proportion to the benefits they provide those requiring assistance. Throw in the benefit to the giver of all those warm smiles, kind words of thanks, and the warm fuzzy feelings that result, and angel activities are a businessman's or investor's dream - all benefits, negligible cost; all return, negligible investment. Furthermore, as one continually has one's antennas up, looking for opportunities to serve, a commitment to the Angel Corps increases one's powers of observation, one's sensitivity to one's surroundings, and one's decision-making abilities. It's starting to sound wonderful, is it not?

But there is an added benefit to joining the Corps. Like the Marine Corps I named it after, the Angel Corps looks out for its own. Through your commitment to joining, you ensure that at the times in your life when you are in need of help, the Corps will have your back. It might come in the form of a person showing up at just the right moment, or it might come as a faceless, fortuitous turn of events. By joining the Corps you connect to something bigger than yourself. Far from a simple quid pro quo, the Corps' commitment to you is integral to its goals and purposes. The Angel Corps embodies the necessity of putting others first, often. There is no greater path to personal happiness, and no greater hope for the future of the planet. Personally, I believe that the Angel Corps just might be the most powerful organization operating anywhere in the world. More powerful than the military might of governments, or the economic might of Wall Street; heck, maybe even more powerful than television! But it can become even more powerful. It needs *you*.

What About Those Harps?

Are there any *real* angels in the Angel Corps? With wings and halos? Would a lack of belief in such prevent secularists /atheists / agnostics, etc. from signing up? A statistic that is frequently used to show how 'irrational' Americans are is the percentage of U.S. citizens who believe in angels. To some, the figure is shockingly, and distressingly, high. Yet many people, throughout history and all over the world, have felt, strongly, that some of the quintessential moments of their lives, the major turning points and so forth, were somehow 'guided'. I don't see that as an irrational position to hold, by any means. I think of an 'angel' as being more like a verb than a noun. Angel means commitment. To serve, to help, to guide. To act when called upon. To put others first. Wings and halo optional.

Perhaps, as it seems to me, the Angel Corps is a universal force; one we strengthen by our participation in it. Certainly, there are many powerful forces surrounding and influencing us. Some, like radio waves, we not only understand, but have learned how to use. The waves have always been there, but we have only known about them - and how to use them - for a hundred years, and change. Others, like the quantum field, are only beginning to be understood. And I'm pretty sure there are others that we haven't discovered yet, exerting influences on our lives even as their presence awaits future discovery.

So, I think it is unrealistic to think of humans as occupying the 'top end' of the Angel Corps, any more than thinking we occupy the pinnacle of evolution. Evolution is an ongoing process, of Life, which we humans are temporarily caught up in. It is like a shifting pattern, a dance of extraordinary configurations. There may be beings well advanced of us living on other planets, and there may be such beings in our own distant future. Like forces that haven't been discovered yet, such as gravity before Newton, their existence wouldn't be contingent upon our awareness of them. If for example, the middle aged person I am now were able to go back in time, and, armed with greater awareness of certain outcomes and consequences, guide a much younger me at crucial points in the younger me's life, I almost certainly would (at times I even wonder, have I?). I think one of the reasons I am drawn to the calling of teacher is that it gives me a chance to - after a fashion - do precisely that. In many ways, the young people I teach are more like my younger self than I am now. The harder the price paid in the learning of a lesson, the greater the value of sharing it, and many of my lessons were learned with the gloves off.

Personally, I believe that all human members of the Corp. have been guided and assisted at times throughout their lives, by 'beings' (actually, in keeping with my notion of angels as verbs, 'doings' might be more fitting) of a higher nature. I can state this about myself with a great deal of certainty, as some of the stories that follow will illustrate.

But I wouldn't want anyone to withhold their participation because they don't share that belief. The benefits of joining the Corps, to oneself and to others, are too wonderful. The difference that joining the Corps can have on one's life is too profound. For heaven's sake (pun intended), no lines should be drawn around how one sees, or refuses to see, 'angels'. No doubt, some of the Corp's wisest and most reliable members reject the notion of any sort of supernatural element guiding their actions. One's dedication to the Corps can derive from secular, humanist principles, or from a desire to model one's live after Christ, or to become a bodhisattva. etc.; the principle is the same; membership requires but one thought, and one commitment: When I am called upon, I will serve. I'm in.

'Angel Moments'

My first year as a Cub Scout. I was very excited about an upcoming event called "The Pinewood Derby". The members of my troop received kits containing a wooden frame, nails, plastic wheels, etc. With these, we were to fashion little cars. We would race them, by rolling them down a long wooden ramp on "Derby Night" six weeks later. I really went to work on my car. A workbench in a corner of the basement contained an array of rusty old tools my dad had used before he passed away: rusty hammer, rusty sander, rusty vise, etc. To my mom they were as incomprehensible as if they had come from another planet, and had gone unused and untended until I decided I needed them to build my car. From upstairs, I brought down some paints and accessories left over from plastic model kits that I or my older brother had worked on.

Lacking a clear concept of what I wanted my car to look like, I nonetheless dove in and sanded and sawed and filed and painted. Eventually I decided I wanted a duotone finish (or, more likely, I just ran out of one color of paint), so the finished product was blue in the front and back and red in the middle. The final result was, putting it charitably, a mess. Tacky fingerprints, uneven sanding, assymetrical cuts, etc. Nevertheless, it was mine. It was my first attempt at crafting something, and as such I was quite proud of it, and rather oblivious to its flaws. I envisioned myself unveiling it with pride to my fellow cubs on Derby Night, perhaps even nabbing a prize. As a somewhat hubristic finishing touch, I took a little silver plastic trophy from one of the plastic model's boxes, and attached it to the car's front with plastic cement.

Derby Night came. We cubs all unveiled our cars as we sat at a large table. The other boys had clearly gotten help. All around me, fine workmanship, such as one wouldn't expect from a nine or ten year old boy, was on display. In particular, my best friend Greg's car was a sleek, stunning beauty, a credit to his father Don's woodworking and carpentry skills. I wasn't particularly deflated - yet - and felt no need to compare my car's amateurishness with the polish of the others; it was mine and I was proud of it. One of my friends admired the trophy adornment. Stoked, I proclaimed in a hammy voice, "This trophy will not stand unless I bring home a trophy tonight!" Truer, more prophetic words were never spoken, as it turned out. My poor, creaky car fell apart on its way down the ramp! The front wheels came off almost at the start. This caused what remained of the 'car' to pop off its groove and fall off the side from a height of perhaps five feet. Sure enough, as it crashed upon the floor, the plastic trophy broke off. Pride went before a fall. Having to pick up that little broken trophy from the floor just added insult to injury.

I felt like a boxer who got KO'd in the first round. But, thinking that boys are not permitted to show that, I did my best to laugh it off in front of my friends. However, a few minutes before it was time to leave, and just before males large and small would be heading toward the cloak room to reclaim their coats, I went into it to create a bit of privacy for myself. There, I started bawling my eyes out. Once the first tears exited their ducts, I couldn't control the outpour. All the unspoken, unresolved pain of going through childhood as a son without a father, of feeling so cheated and denied, came pouring out of me at once, a dam break that had been set off by the evening's humiliation. Crouching in that cloakroom, I knew that I would eventually be discovered, and envisioned a crowd of boys laughing at me. Still, I couldn't stop crying. It was a blessing that Don, Greg's father, was the person who came upon me hunched over myself in a corner. He didn't say a word, but awkwardly made some noises to make me aware of his presence, thereby giving me a chance to pull myself together. Because of his kind gesture, no one else, not even Greg, knew about my breakdown in the cloak room, and nothing was ever said about it from the one person who had witnessed it. As our homes were just a block apart, Don gave me a ride home. Just before dropping me off, he turned round to me in the backseat and said, "Next year, Andy, bring your kit over to our house. You, me and Greg can work on both cars together".

In that cloakroom, Don experienced what I have come to recognize as an 'angel moment': a situation where a person comes across another in need, and who that person is being called upon to assist, as best as he or she can. It is as if life chose that very person for that very moment. Circumstances arranged it that they, and not another, would show up at that place, in that time, and in that capacity. Not all take the opportunity, but all will assuredly experience it at points throughout their lives. It could have been anyone who happened upon me bawling in the cloakroom; another dad, or one of my fellow scouts. The outcome would likely have been very different, and possibly much more humiliating. The fact is, Don was the ideal person to find me there. He possessed just the right quality of quiet compassion, and he followed his instincts perfectly. He was 'in'. As a finishing stroke, he chose to offer his help in building the next year's car, thus going beyond the call of duty. Without that, I likely would have decided that I would never put myself through that ordeal again. He raised me up to more than I could be, as the song goes. Such is the power of angel moments, and what makes them so important.

As it turned out, the following year Don's support went beyond even his offer to me in the car (as I'll describe). This, I believe, is another signature of an 'angel moment'. As a result of having offered assistance in some way, we forge a deeper connection to the person we have helped. They come to occupy a space in our heart. Even if we never see that person again, *they* have helped *us*, by expanding an essential chamber in our hearts, where compassion dwells. And thus a vital link is formed between the helper and the helped.

Those days spent working with Don and Greg in Don's wondrous workshop (the polar opposite of the dusty/rusty/musty table I had worked on the year before) were a time of great joy for me, brimming with possibility. Having lost my own father at two, I had never experienced what it was like to be mentored by a male elder before. Don did most of the work on the cars, while Greg and I spent most of the time cracking each other up, as best friends will. Still, we were frequently called upon by Don to choose designs and colors, and provide finishing touches (with his supervision) to the sanding, painting and molding of our two cars, in order for us to be able to claim credit for the final results. Greg's was a sleek, metallic blue beauty that could have rescued a heroine in a science fiction movie. Mine was more of a retro number, recalling racing cars from the early 20th century. Its crowning feature was its front grill; a row of finely chiseled shark's teeth. To me, it was the coolest thing in the world, and my most prized possession.

Our two cars got the most envious gazes, both from the other cubs and their dads. However, by the luck of the draw, my car was placed on an end track when its turn to race came up, and that particular track had been slowing down cars all night. So, it ended up not winning its race, instead coming in second. As for the design competition, although I am sure that my car received consideration, the top prize ended up going to Greg's futuristic wonder, to nobody's surprise. Thus, even though the evening had exceeded my wildest expectations, and completely wiped out the memory of the previous year's debacle, I went home empty handed in the prizes department.

So, what did Don do next? As an angel, he felt that something more was needed, and promptly acted upon that feeling. He headed straight to his workshop, and crafted for me my very own trophy, a 'runner's up' trophy for both design and speed, and delivered it to my home the following day. Nothing official about it; it was purely a gesture from his heart. But, like my car, it was a finely crafted masterpiece, the equal of any of the trophies that had been presented the night before. My mother proudly displayed it on the living room mantle, and it remained there for years. Don had deftly performed an angel's task; he had done everything he could to make me, an insecure and awkward boy, feel special, and capable.

My own decisive 'angel moment' came many years later, when I was a young man, living in California with my wife and baby daughter. It was, in fact, the experience that initiated me into the Corps; the moment when I began to sprout my very own wings. It was October, 1991. We lived in a large apartment complex high in the hills of Oakland, directly above the southern edge of the University of California, Berkeley, where my wife was studying. The San Francisco Bay Area was enduring the fifth year of one of its many droughts. A small forest fire that had quickly been extinguished on Saturday, the previous day, had instilled a tinge of nervousness in the residents of the Oakland Hills. I remember joking with the guard at the entrance to our complex, as I headed out that Saturday, asking him 'will there be a place to come back to?' Which, there was. *That* day.

Sunday morning, I woke up around eight, and stepped out to pick up the newspaper. I had a very brief, friendly conversation with another one of the residents, Donna, a woman about my age. Although she lived just across the hall, this was our first opportunity to introduce ourselves. That encounter was the first of its kind the eight months I'd been living there. All that time, but I had never spoken to a person in the hallway before. The only other residents I'd ever conversed with were by the pool or at the gym. It was a place where everyone kept different hours, and it was rare to see anyone.

Donna and I wished each other a good day. I went in with the newspaper, and my wife and I began making pancakes. By eleven, a smoky haze was visible outside, just as it had been the day before. Either an ember from Saturday's fire had survived, or, more troubling, in the case of deliberate arson, the perpetrator had started *another* fire, dissatisfied with the dimensions achieved by his previous efforts. In either case, this fire was a different beast altogether. The drought had turned the thirsty eucalyptus trees that filled the hills into match-ready timber, and the fire grew to gigantic proportions with frightening alacrity. I was shocked to see a row of houses along the ridge above our complex explode, one after the other, as if they were nothing more than popcorn kernels in a kettle. It is almost a hallucinatory experience to watch a house, repository of decades of memorabilia and experiences, pop out of existence like that. One would think all those dimensions of human experience held within them would give them greater solidity, somehow. But, no.

A hasty call to 911 was met on the other side with near disbelief. Get. Out. NOW! was the blunt message I received from the lady who fielded my call. So, we grabbed our nine month old baby, such necessary papers and so forth as we could get our hands on (including a stack of pastel drawings of mine), and hurried down to the parking garage in the basement of our building. The sight before us as we pulled out from the garage was far more horrifying than we had anticipated. The earlier view from our window hadn't shown us that, from the opposite direction, the fire had encroached to just behind our building. An eerily billowing curtain of flames, perhaps two hundred feet high, hung menacingly over the entire complex.

Our car joined the queue squeezing out the complex's only exit. The queue was orderly, fortunately. Laid back Californians, accustomed to traffic jams, behave themselves, even in circumstances as threatening as the one we were all facing. When my car was perhaps the tenth or so back from the exit gate, I caught something just out the corner of my eye, over to my right. Several firetrucks were parked on the lawn at the entrance to the complex, and firefighters were making an (ultimately futile, as the entire complex soon thereafter burned to the ground) attempt to stave off the fire. Just beside them, I noticed a young woman, looking frantic. Somehow, though it happened in a flash, I sensed that she direly needed passage out of there. Otherwise she'd have to stay with the firefighters until they had completed their task, or were forced to escape themselves.

I pulled the car out of the queue, so as not to disrupt its flow, and opened the door on the passenger side. My wife was in back with the baby. I could read the woman's facial expressions precisely, as she quickly analyzed her options, made her decision, and got inside. The driver behind me had observed what transpired, and with a friendly wave, allowed me back in line. Another angel. The whole episode lasted perhaps no more than eight seconds.

As we drove down the hill, toward safety, I realized that my new passenger was Donna, the very same woman I had met earlier that day in the hallway. A neighbor of mine for eight months, yet I'd seen her only once before - that very day - and just prior to our current, far less mundane, encounter. She explained that she stood near the firefighters in hopes that her husband, who had already headed into town that day, would be able to get back to our complex and get her out of there. Her hesitation to get in the car with us was out of concern that he would reach the complex and lose precious time searching for her. As it turned out, there was no way that would have happened, as all upward heading traffic (what little there was of that) was stopped at the base of the hill by firefighters and police, to create more lanes for descending cars to escape by.

I had never seen myself as a 'rescuer' of any kind, and miles away from being considered a hero. Had Donna needed any other type of 'heroics', such as those requiring martial arts skills, weapons training, snake bite treatment, etc., I would have been of no use whatsoever. Even in this particular case, I surprised myself by how quick my decision making had been. Up to that point, I thought of myself as the type of person who would drive halfway down the hill before thinking, 'you know what? I think I saw somebody back there. I wonder if I should have let her in the car...?' Not *unwilling* to help, just not the type to make snap decisions when called upon. Yet, in that instance, in order to be of assistance - perhaps even to save a life - all I needed was a car, and a quick response. That much I was capable of. The fact that I had just met Donna a couple hours ago, and was now escorting her from an inferno, made it seem as if the whole episode had been somehow scripted, for both of us. In retrospect, I think perhaps the Angel Corps was 'recruiting' me, curious to see whether or not I had what it took to join. Just as Greg's father Don, long ago, had been guided by the Corps; the one person - out of many possible people - to come upon me in that cloakroom, and provide redemption to the situation.

The drive down the hill was a scene out of a nightmare. The forest beyond the edge of the road was ablaze on both sides, bringing flames right to the curbs. Behind us: the inferno that I saw when pulling out of the parking garage. In front of us: an invisible road, completely obscured by smoke. Our only option was to drive into, and through, an eerie wall of blackness that looked like the entrance to hell. None of us in the car, or in the cars in front and back of us, could be certain that we weren't driving straight *into* the fire. In a brief moment of sheer panic, I wanted to simply put on the brakes right there and stop. Like a deer caught in headlights, my mind instinctively rejected the option of driving into a wall of smoke, even though all other choices meant certain death.

I resisted the instinct, and braced myself to head into the darkness. Then, an extraordinary thing happened. I clearly heard the voice of a man, as if another passenger had suddenly popped into the seat next to me. With an air of absolute confidence, the voice assured me, 'everything will be okay.' It was unlike anything I had ever experienced. Yet, rather than freaking me out, the sudden voice had a calming effect. I felt that I could trust both it, and its message. Partly as a reflex, partly to reassure myself, I parroted what I had just been 'told' (in a far shakier voice). Those same exact four words, nothing more, as our car became enveloped by the smoke. "Everything will be okay".

For probably no more than six or seven seconds - but seeming much longer - we drove through almost complete darkness, with nothing visible beyond a faint view of the car directly in front of us through the headlights. Then, slowly, the blackness thinned, and eventually we had a steadily clearer view of the city of Berkeley below, and of the great city across the bay, finally to the welcome sight of Mt. Tamalpais in the distance, sleeping unperturbed. As our lane merged with others, the highway filled with cars speeding down the hill toward safety. Everyone in the car breathed sighs of relief (excepting the baby, who slept blissfully unaware throughout the whole adventure), realizing we were going to survive. Donna began to speak animatedly. "I was *so* scared back then! When we drove into that smoke, I really thought we were going to die! But as soon as you said, 'everything will be okay', I calmed down. I trusted that we'd make it."

That was surprising. When I had spoken, my voice was cracked and weak, nothing like the confident voice I was mimicking. I wouldn't have thought it had a particularly reassuring tone. But the effect on Donna was the same as that of the voice I had heard had on me. It was as if the words were like a spell of some kind, and as I relayed them, my own voice was imbued with a kind of totemic power. Although at the time, I would have been hard pressed to explain exactly why I felt the need to speak them out loud, looking back I feel that perhaps it was because they were not meant for me alone; it was a message that everyone in the car (even the baby, in some way perhaps) needed to hear.

I wasn't a believer then, nor did the experience serve to 'convert' me, in the conventional meaning of that word. I certainly didn't think the voice belonged to Jesus, as others raised in Christian households may have, or to any other religious figure. On the other hand, the eight months leading up to that experience; of being a father, of watching the amazing process of a baby developing from little more than a ruddy, potato-like sack into a powerful, unique individual, had profoundly shaped my outlook. I was neither an atheist nor a religious person before the Oakland fire, and the same held true the following day, despite the mysterious 'voice' I had heard and relayed. But I was, at the very least, 'opened' by the extraordinary nature of the episode. I was willing to consider that any number of explanations for what happened on that day may have held. Such an extraordinary coincidence to have seen Donna just that one time, a few hours earlier. Was that why I caught her out the corner of my eye? Had her appearance somehow imprinted itself upon my mind? As for the 'voice', what *was* it? I didn't have an answer, but I wasn't willing to simply dismiss it as the effect of adrenaline, or a message from my subconscious. I wasn't going to denude the experience of its power or significance by reducing it to such.

The most satisfying way for me to consider that episode, looking back on it, was that I was being recruited by the Angel Corps. I was given an opportunity to perform a 'heroic' task, though I had no particular ability with which to do so other than being able to drive a car. Up until that time, I had benefitted from the angelic tasks of others more times than I could count. Some I remembered, others I didn't. And there were undoubtedly other times in my life when I had played the role of somebody else's angel, though none so memorable or dramatic. Perhaps the episode amounted to a test (a baptism by fire?). Was I willing to be an initiate? I could, of course, have just driven on, assuming the firefighters would take care of Donna, or someone else in the queue would eventually give her a lift. I could have, as I wrote above, driven halfway down the hill, briefly regretted not stopping for her, and thereupon forgotten all about it. I like to think that some of the Corps' recruiters were watching to see what I would do. I also feel that my life would have ended up on different, perhaps very different, trajectories, based upon how I made that split decision. By stopping the car, I was demonstrating to the Corps that I was 'in'.

We drove with Donna all the way to the home of friends who were living in Berkeley. They put us up – and put up with us – until we were able to get campus housing from UC. Donna was able to get in touch with her husband from our friends' place, and he quickly arrived to take her to their own temporary home, with relatives.

We all hugged, and said our goodbyes. I never saw Donna again. Such is often the case; angel moments play out as the briefest passings of ships in the night. An angel fulfills his or her role, and promptly exits the scene. Others, as was the case with Don, establish, or serve to cement, bonds that last a lifetime.

Midway between my experiences with Don and with Donna, another one, of the former type, profoundly influenced the direction my life would ultimately take. A very special angel played an instrumental role in rescuing me from the lowest period of my life. During my late adolescence and early adulthood, I suffered from low self esteem, and often felt empty and isolated. I slacked. I worked a variety of unfulfilling part time jobs while attending art school, and for a period after graduating. I failed to rise to, or even recognize, the opportunities my talent and creativity presented. Instead, I drank, and experimented a bit with drugs. Such 'self medicating' was often the only way I was able to lighten my mood.

One such night of mood lightening, I was partying with a coworker from one of my dead-end jobs. Unlike me, who was basically a dabbler, he was a chronic substance abuser, perhaps even an addict. I had never dropped acid (or whatever it was) previously, but he kept shoving pills at me and downing them himself, and as I grew higher I completely abandoned self control and allowed him to be the evening's maestro. In the back of my head I knew I was taking a terrible risk, as he seemed up for any excess. Inevitably, the 'trip' went bad, and my hallucinations took on a sinister and terrifying tone. There were a couple houseplants in his apartment that he took no better care of than he did his own body. They had possibly never been watered. I stared across the room at these two withering specimens. Both were dying. The taller wilted over, and onto, the smaller one. The larger plant looked to me like an evil, mantis-like creature that was sucking the life out of its helpless prey. My coworker began to appear similarly mantis-like, sucking the life out of me. I freaked out, and sensed I needed to get out of there immediately, that perhaps even my life was on the line. Without explanation, I bolted out of his apartment, and got in my car.

I was in no condition to drive across town - or even a few blocks for that matter - but I hoped that if I avoided the freeway I would be okay. A long stretch of High Street, Columbus' main thoroughfare, lay between me and home. As I drove along, I could see the lights change from green to red, and could feel my foot press down on the brake. But, even as I knew I had stopped, the car and everything else seemed to keep moving. The streets, the buildings, everything seemed to speed both toward me and away from me. Everything, that is, but the red traffic lights, which taunted me, like the "eye" of HAL in 2001. They remained fixed in front of my eyes. I knew the car was stopped, yet still felt like I was speeding down the street.

At around the third stoplight, I grew afraid that I would never make it home alive if I kept on like that. I gave up on getting home that night, and pulled over onto a dark side street. It was around three in the morning. I stretched out on the car seat, and fitfully slept. When I woke up at around eight, I looked out the window and got a surprise. Without realizing, I had parked my car directly in front of a church.

I had little use for churches, and hadn't for many years. But my childhood experiences with them had taught me that, at the very least, the priest or pastor or whoever was inside was duty bound to give an ear to a soul in need. Which is what I was. I was at, or near, the lowest point in my life, had zero self esteem, and needed to talk to somebody. Like a medieval peasant shouting 'sanctuary!', I dragged myself in and eventually located the pastor, an elderly man with silver hair and thick spectacles. He listened kindly and patiently to my tale of woe, despite not really comprehending, as I was so stoned that my words were nearly incoherent. What I did get him to understand was that I wanted desperately to get home and into bed, but was in no condition to drive myself there. He called the church's caretaker and told him to give me a ride home in the church's small truck. He wrote down the church's address for me so I could find my way back, and come for my own car later.

The caretaker arrived. He was a gentle and warm-hearted man of perhaps sixty. Surely, he was quite capable of performing the chores that his job required, which included driving. Yet it was obvious, even to me in the state I was in, that he suffered from a rather pronounced mental disability, perhaps as a result of an injury suffered in childhood. We chatted, he through a speech impediment (and I through my own temporary one), as I gave him directions to my home. As I sat in the passenger seat, it suddenly dawned on me that I was wasting my life. I was wasting all my talents and gifts. I was a mere passenger, in more ways than one, and as such was allowing life, my one and only, to pass me by. And, through my own irresponsibility I had reached the point where I needed to be chauffeured home by someone who had not been given the gifts that I was foolishly squandering. Someone who, at least in some ways, had far less than I - a man who had probably spent a large portion of his life in special needs schools, training programs, and so forth. Someone who the church had probably hired through such a program.

This was a deeply humbling, even humiliating, experience for me. I felt compassion toward my 'angel' in the driver's seat, cognizant of the fact that life was probably very difficult for him at times. Yet in that moment it was I, not he, who felt - and was - truly disabled, through my own self destructiveness, and just plain foolishness. There he was, making the best use of what he'd been given, providing help and service to others in the process. And there I was, wasting what I'd been given, and running from life down dead end streets. More than merely a driver, he was my deliverer. Not only did he safely deliver me home that day; more importantly, he taught me a crucial life lesson in that truck, just by being who he was. As I lay in bed all that day, depressed and disoriented, the lesson sank in hard.

From that very day, I began to take steps that would in due course turn my life around. It started with saying goodbye to the drugs, and 'friends' like my coworker. Over the course of the ensuing days, I often turned that episode over in my head. I was willing to accept the possibility that I had been guided, somehow. Every aspect of the situation seemed tailor-made to bring home to me precisely the lessons that my future, if I was to have one, depended on. The firm decision to stop the car, the coincidence of parking in front of the church, the caretaker's disability, my sudden realization in the passenger's seat; it all had seemed guided and purposeful. Perhaps it was the Corps at work?

In all three of the angel moments described above, the benefit to the receiver was of a completely different order than the simple acts of services rendered. Although I can't speak for Donna, in both cases where I was the one in need of assistance (it is ironic that all three events involve cars - something about deliverance?) my life switched over to a better trajectory through the actions of my two angels. This is something that neither of them would have anticipated. Their actions were perhaps quickly forgotten by them, their significance never fully grasped. And yet the effect on me was profound. It wouldn't surprise me to learn that, in some way, Donna, too, received more than just a ride down a hill that day, perhaps something longer lasting. I have come to know angel moments as possessing a very deep and moving quality.

Just think how many such acts are being performed each day, and of the profound life lessons, and expanded opportunities, that result. None of us ever knows just how, or when, we may play an instrumental role in changing someone's life for the better. What I do know is that these moments occur far more than we imagine. Perhaps you, yourself, have been involved in an angel moment just recently. Or perhaps you will tomorrow.

Our Duties to Smaller Ones

The sight of baked, shriveled worms on a pavement after a rainy day is never a welcome one. Our two species being so different, we can't really know how the worms themselves experience such an undignified death. Do they panic when they lose all sense of direction, and every frantic wriggle leads to nowhere? Do they experience agony, as a relentless sun slowly grafts them to the ground? There is no question that, to a certain degree - and to the only degree that matters to them - they suffer. And let's be honest; it is our human-constructed world that causes these tragic deaths. The paved, slick, car friendly surfaces we build are not something the worms are equipped to traverse. The surface of the earth that they are evolved for and accustomed to is porous, one they are able to navigate like a hippo does water; up, down, in, out. Forgiving. They meet their fates on an unforgiving surface that would seem to them to have been created by a cruel madman. *What is this place?*, I imagine them wondering.

So, we owe worms. Indeed, they look messy on the street,

but they are our mess. They die on our surfaces, laid for our convenience; surfaces as alien to them as an acre of Venus would be to us. One of the simplest acts a member of the Angel Corps can perform, and one of the most common, I suspect (though you will rarely hear the matter pop up in conversation) is to protect these humble creatures where and when we can. Simply pick them up, when you come upon them in the midst of their predicaments, and place them where they belong. In, or upon, soil. Perhaps place a little soil on top of them so they can revive more rapidly. We can't save them all, and indeed we might not even be able to save most of the ones we do pick up, but like all Angel Corps acts, that shouldn't discourage us, nor does it diminish the value of saving one, two, or as many as we can. Even the ones that don't make it; doesn't it seem that they would prefer to die on the familiar territory of moist soil, something they can recognize, something that welcomes them? Surely we can give them a (hopefully) less painful, more dignified, and natural way to die.

What is the cost to us? Well, some people just find the very thought of picking up a worm to be revolting. To them, I could only suggest: do it anyway. It might be revolting, at first, but surely the feeling wears off with practice. Their slime is extremely sticky, so whatever dirt you get on your fingers during your rescue mission will stay there for a while. It might take a bit of self-persuading if, for example, you are on your way to an interview, or a date. The livelier ones might well freak you out. Not guessing your intent, they are likely to thrash about with an energy you hadn't guessed they possessed. They might escape your grip several times before you get them to a safe spot, and you may just want to give up on the frenzied ingrates. On the other hand, those are probably the ones with the best chance of survival once you do manage to get them back where they belong, so your perseverance will pay off. In all cases, the point is that the cost is so utterly minuscule in comparison to the enormity of the act you are performing, from the perspective of the worm. Before you arrived at the scene, it had no alternative to a slow, excruciating death. But now, because of you, it is returned to life, or at least the gift of dying in a more familiar and friendly, and less painful and humiliating, setting. Think how much such a gift would mean to you. That is the essence of the Angel Corps in a nutshell.

In my own case, I see rescuing worms as a repayment of karmic debt. From the ages of eight to perhaps thirteen, it was a summer rite of passage for my older brother and I to venture out into the backyard at night, armed with flashlights, in search of 'nightcrawlers' that we would place in a coffee can and use as bait on the following day's fishing excursion. These were senseless murders, as we rarely caught anything. I still remember how the worms reacted to the shock of being placed on a hook, writhing about in agony, and their withered, gray corpses as I pulled what remained of them out of the water. I gradually grew more and more mortified by what I was doing, which led me to give up fishing entirely. Towards the end of my fishing career, I would only pretend to place the worms on a hook. Out of my brother's (and whoever else we happened to be fishing with) sight, I would set them free, and cast my hook and sinker into the water un-baited (with barely a perceptible change in the result, such was my lack of fishing prowess to begin with). When all is said and done, I may never end up saving as many worms as I killed in my childhood, but I consider each rescue a tiny act of atonement.

Rescuing animals from other animals, or from nature itself, is of course a different thing. In the case of worms on a pavement, clearly the roads are the culprits. However, the rhythms of the natural world present a vastly different, and more complex, scenario. Animals do need to eat other animals in order to survive themselves. A mother frog produces thousands of eggs so that only a lucky few can make it out of the tadpole stage, while the majority simply nourish various predators. Nestlings fall out of trees. Floods wipe out whole ecosystems, claiming millions of lives. Nature can be, and often is, very harsh, and that will never change. In the cases where we decide to rescue, for example, prey from predator, we are not righting a wrong. We are simply responding to the evocation of pity that issues from our hearts.

I recall a scene many years ago, as I walked along a river near my home in suburban Tokyo, surrounded by high grasses and a scattering of thin trees. Along the narrow, seasonal path local fisherman had carved, before the growing frenzy of early summer made it impassable, I came upon a large black beetle, stuck in a spider's web and completely immobilized under a gauze of intertwining threads. I stopped, and quickly noticed the spider that had trapped it nearby, about the same size as its prey. My trudging along the path had startled it, and it had fled to a lower corner of its large web, from where it watched me intently.

Though the beetle was almost completely immobilized within its tightly wound sarcophagus, it was making faint, pathetic motions in a hopeless attempt to free itself. I picked it up, and considered what to do. Meanwhile, the spider never took its (many) eyes off me. Had it been an easy matter to make a tear in the cocoon, and pull it off in one or two motions, I certainly would have done so. But a few attempts at this proved utterly futile. Spiders trap their prey through a meticulous procedure that is not easily undone. So, I set upon the only possible course, which was to unravel the threads one after the other. I wasn't even sure if there was any point to my effort; the beetle was so nearly motionless that it might well have already been near death. As thorough as the spider had been in doing its work, I had to be even more so in undoing it, as clumsy motions could easily have torn off one of the beetle's appendages.

When one rescues very small creatures, one must deal with the possibility that we might, in some cases, be actually making things worse, not better. If I had done serious damage to the beetle while trying to free it, I might have increased its suffering without altering the outcome in any way.

Once, to my horror, I had placed a very weakened worm upon a patch of soil, only to have it almost instantly set upon by a ravenous horde of tiny ants. I pulled it off and placed it elsewhere, but not before it had to endure the pain of hundreds of bites. I doubt the creature lived much longer; had I only compounded its misery? So, I worked as methodically and patiently as I could. I probably worked as long unraveling the beetle as the spider worked at raveling it. Altogether, it took about forty five minutes under a hot June sun. All the while, the spider watched me. What was going through its head, I wondered. It was powerless to do anything but watch the meal it had worked so hard to capture being taken away from it. As I worked, I made 'small talk' to both creatures. To the beetle I gave reassurances, while to the spider I was gently scolding. "I understand that you have to eat, and I'm sorry to be doing this. But your hunting methods are cruel, and I'm not about to walk by and let this poor creature suffer." I actually considered destroying the spider's enormous trap, making it work even harder for its next victim, but how could I, while it perched there, watching me in utter defeat? Spiders gotta eat.

Finally, the last few threads gave way. Fortunately, the beetle appeared not to have been damaged. Its earlier movements had been so feeble because it couldn't move. Now freed, it straightened itself out on my fingertip, and after a half a minute or so, extended its wings, and burst into flight. Triumphantly, I watched it fly over my head and out of sight, given a new lease on life. Now there was just me and the spider. We gave each other one last look (and I'll make no conjecture as to how the spider felt about me at the time) and I continued on with my walk.

Another episode by the river (that river, the Tama, has been the stage of so many memorable moments in my life they could fill a book), around the same time, required even greater effort on my part, and ended rather more ambiguously. The environment along its banks are continually being altered by the landscaping work of the heavy rains of late summer. Tiny islands and ponds appear and disappear, sometimes lasting a year or two, sometimes lasting only a matter of weeks. Every time a new feature appears on the landscape, animals gather around and fill in the spaces; they hunt, produce offspring, etc. I remember a lovely pond I passed by for perhaps three or more years. Dozens of turtles made it their home, and I often saw them basking on logs or poking their heads above the surface of the pond. One year the rains came so hard and lasted so long that the pond was permanently rejoined with the river; all land between the two bodies of water was washed away for good. I have no idea what happened to the turtles, and haven't seen any since. I miss the days when I could circumnavigate that pond on my walk (it was particularly gorgeous in winter when it froze, and a misty pillow rose from it in the early morning). Yet, I know that if the pond ever returns, so will the turtles. Such is the way of things along the Tama.

One late summer, on a sunny day that followed several rainy ones, I received another angel call to duty. As I walked along the trail, at a slight elevation from the river's bank, I heard a very strange sound; quite a hubbub, in fact. It was odd to hear any loud noises along this fairly isolated path used only by myself and the men who fished the river. I'd certainly never heard anything like this before. The sound grew as I drew closer, until at last I came upon its source. A very small, very shallow body of water had been created by the rains, which had now receded, trapping dozens of enormous carp who could no longer access the river twenty yards away. They were panicking as they gasped for air, quickly draining the 'pond' of its oxygen by their sheer numbers. The sound I heard was their frantic splashing. I couldn't just leave them there, but what was I supposed to do?

I looked around to see if there was something I could put them in, in order to transport them to the river. For the only time in my life, I was glad that people tended to use the river as a dumping ground (and heavy rains always deposited a fresh, hideous assortment of junk, such as bicycle handles, styrofoam containers, plastic bags, etc., along its banks), because I quickly found a large, still intact, styrofoam container about the size of a child's wagon. I calculated that it could hold about four or five carp at a go, not yet realizing how difficult it would be to get, and keep, even one fish in there, nor how heavy this container would get with that many fish and a bit of water in it!

Unlike the many worms I have saved, which have only minuscule strength in comparison to a human's, or the helpless beetle wrapped up like a mummy, those fish were strong! And they had no idea whatsoever that I was trying to help. All they wanted to do was get away from me! Even though the 'pond' was tiny, it nevertheless gave them enough maneuvering room to continually evade me. And even after I managed to get one from the water to the styrofoam tub, as often as not it quickly wriggled out. The most I ever managed to get into the tub at one time, through a huge amount of effort, was three, and even then my task was far from completed. Because the twenty yards or so of uneven terrain I had to cover to reach the river in order to release them gave them plenty of time to wriggle out en route. And by the time I managed to pick up one flopping resister and get it back in the tub, another had gotten loose. Thus, even after the first two trips, I was completely exhausted, filthy, and dripping with sweat. And I smelled like fish. I cursed many a curse at these silly creatures who were so determined to get free from me that they were willing to jump out onto dry land!

I recognized that I wasn't doing myself any favors by attempting to transport more than one at a time, as they were so unmanageable in larger numbers. On top of which, my arms were already feeling weak. Over the course of about an hour, one by one, I managed to save just over half the fish. I had walked back and forth from the river to the pond so many times, and fallen a few times as well, that I could hardly walk anymore. My legs were shaking, my back ached, and my arms had lost most of their strength. Making matters worse, by now the pond had emptied out substantially, making it nearly impossible to rescue any more fish. They simply had too much space to maneuver in. Thus, total exhaustion, awareness that I had an appointment in my real life coming up shortly that I really couldn't be late for (and couldn't go to smelling like a rotting fish), and the sheer futility of saving any more of them, caused me to leave the job half done. With great sadness, I walked away from the fish I was unable to save, after silently and solemnly apologizing to them. I had been unable to communicate to them that I was there to help, which made my task a hundred times harder. Already panicked by their predicament, they became even more so as I lunged at them with grasping hands, seeming more like a predator than a savior. Their instincts told them to evade me, and sadly, that cost many of them their lives. Still, many had been saved, and I hope those that did went on to live long, happy lives.

In referring to such actions as 'angel's' work, I by no means wish to equate them with the actions of those who dedicate their lives to bettering conditions of animals; volunteering in shelters and taking part in other rescue activities, organizing and participating in protests against the horrific treatment animals receive in factory farms, in many zoos and water parks, in bull fights, etc. The decision to become a vegan is another commitment one can make toward relieving animal suffering that I consider 'angelic'. The fact is, we humans have treated animals horribly century after century, and those people who dedicate their time and resources toward righting so many of these wrongs should be seen as angels who have truly earned their stripes, while I remain a buck private in comparison. There are different ways each of us defines 'hero', but such people are true heroes in my book, and they are performing some of the Angel Corps' most important work in the world.

Yet, humbler activities such as saving worms, or the carp by the river, are also very important. All of us can do something for our fellow creatures. Even if, for whatever reason, we cannot provide a permanent home to an abandoned animal, there are still ways we can help the strays in our midst. Stray cats are generally wary of people, but there are friendly ones as well. Sometimes just spending a few moments with them, stroking their fur and pouring affection on them, can be the most genuine act of service you could perform. Carrying around a bag of dry cat food, so that you always have something to share with them when you cross their paths can be an even more meaningful gesture.

Connecting with animals is important. Our modern society has done all it can to isolate us from our fellow creatures. We have fashioned a world that has become so people-centric that some of us go through whole days without ever seeing another species from the animal kingdom, and often go days without even thinking about them. Recently, I walked into a supermarket with my pet ferret in my bag, and one of the cashiers told me I would have to leave, as animals were not allowed inside. No animals in a supermarket? Just what, I wanted to ask her, did she think they were selling in the meat and fish sections? It is tragic that we have become so disconnected to them, such that we freak out at the mere sight of a spider scurrying across the floor, or a ferret (gasp!) and all its 'germs' in a supermarket. It speaks to how far astray we have wandered.

Is it possible that one of the main reasons there is so much alienation, depression and other forms of mental illness plaguing the human species is because our relationship to our fellow creatures has become so distorted? We are a lonely species. Any action that connects us to animals in a meaningful way, that reminds us of their importance, of their kinship with us on a majestic Tree of Life, that lets us share our love with them, is good. It is one of the best ways we can be as angels upon this earth, and, in the reciprocal nature of angel activity, one of the best things we can do for ourselves.

Try a Little Tenderness

While a toddler, my daughter became friends with two sisters she met at her daycare center. Sakura was a year younger than Mika, and two years behind her was Mirai. Where Mirai fell short in terms of size and development, she made up for in an extra dose of spunk. And – as I have a tendency to root for underdogs - perpetual kid sister Mirai, trying to hang with the big girls, came to occupy a special place in my heart. Besides, children grow up so quickly that I was grateful to have Mirai continue to giggle and gush at the little games and jokes I would play that Mika and Sakura outgrew (and let me know in no uncertain terms that they had outgrown).

Typically, on weekends the three would play together at either home. One Saturday in winter, when the girls were ages seven, six and four (and a baby sister had been added to Sakura and Mirai's family), the inseparable threesome started the day at our home, with plans for Mika to later sleep over at the girls'. It one of those rare days in Tokyo where the snow fell very heavily, approaching a Midwest blizzard in intensity. I don't recall the reason, but Mika and Sakura had already gone to play at Sakura's home earlier, when the snow and wind were less intense, while Mirai had stayed behind. Because Mirai's mother was occupied with her newborn, as well as the older girls, the task fell on me to chaperone her home.

This was hardly angel work; it was just a typical chore such as parents often must perform for their own children, or their children's friends. However, because Mirai was so small, and the snowstorm was so strong, in order to get her home about a half mile away, I needed to place her on my back and trudge through the snow, bent forward against howling, snapping winds like an ancient wayfarer, while she clung on with arms draped over my shoulders. It felt more dramatic than it actually was (it actually wasn't dramatic at all). There was no real danger, but somehow, feeling her behind me, face pressed to my back, I felt transported back to earlier, harsher times when the journeys families took through blizzards were often life or death situations. For that brief moment, I felt fully entrusted with her safety. The grip of her small hands, and the pressure of her body against my back through our thick clothing, communicated more than words could the trust she felt. She relied on me, to shelter her from the storm and deliver her safely home. Though the 'heroic' feelings I felt were merely imitative, another feeling, that I felt toward that little girl who clung to me so trustingly, was not. It was tenderness. I wouldn't have traded the feeling for any other in the world. I felt strongly, deeply connected to her. The feeling reached its climax when I arrived at her home and passed her over into the grateful arms of her mother. It continued as a warm glow inside on my trudge back home.

I experienced that same feeling of tenderness when, by the river, I took great care in releasing the beetle from the spider's cocoon, so as not to snap off legs or wings. I've felt it toward worms I've cradled in my hands while looking for a suitable patch of soil to deposit them in. I imagine that, many years ago, when Don worked with me to heal the pain of my first Pinewood Derby event, he felt it toward me as well. Perhaps his tenderness was implanted in me like a seed that would bloom when I had reached a certain age, and was ready and willing to take responsibility for another's safety or dignity.

Tenderness is one of the profoundest and most beautiful of human emotions. It runs perhaps even deeper than romantic love or friendship. It awakens something powerful, and yet very vulnerable, within us. It can be heartbreaking, but in a way the heart needs to be broken in order for us to live as adults. One of the greatest benefits of joining the Angel Corps is the growing familiarity with tenderness one cultivates through the performance of one's duties.

Tenderness is not an emotion that is especially encouraged in our society. It is rarely even talked about. It is not marketable in the way that pride, competitiveness, sexual desire, etc. are. Corporations that wish to sell us things, and the advertising industry they employ to help them, prefer that we remain in a perpetually adolescent state of fretting about, and tending to, our own desires. Tenderness, the feeling we get when tending to the needs of another, cannot be exploited or manufactured. It can't be given the steroid treatment of a clever advertising campaign. No products to buy, so no reason to try. Part of what makes it so special is precisely that it is so off the grid of corporate manipulation. And yet, that also makes it something that, if we are to experience it (and we should), we must discover for ourselves. And I can think of no better way to do that than through a daily commitment to serve, when called upon.

Committing to the Angel Corps gives us more than the good feelings that go along with helping someone in need. It gives us more than the confidence that we will be similarly looked after when we find ourselves in a jam (and we will; The Corps looks out for its own). The best thing we receive from joining the Corps is the version of ourselves we get to live with: a better version of who we are. Our consciousness lifts. Beautiful experiences and emotions may come upon us at any time, unexpectedly. A feeling that begins as tenderness might expand into an indescribable feeling of gratitude, or intense joy. We might be simply walking along the street on a sunny day, and then, *there it is*. We are suddenly awash in intense and beautiful feelings, and these might last an hour or more. The gratitude we feel for the feeling causes it to grow even stronger. Such moments are among my most precious, and my wish is that everyone can experience them, and often.

LET YOUR LEFT HAND KNOW...

Is it wrong to 'brag' about our Angel Corps activities? As someone who was raised in a Catholic household and attended parochial schools, this is something that I have struggled with. There is a passage in the New Testament, in Matthew, that instructs, "Beware of practicing your righteousness before men to be noticed by them; otherwise you have no reward with your Father who is in heaven. But when you give to the poor, do not let your left hand know what your right hand is doing,…." Like so many of the lessons I was taught by the well meaning people who nurtured my spirituality, that admonition has stuck with me, as I am sure it has for many people.

Yet, if we adhere to a strict policy that all our 'angelic' acts are carried out covertly, mightn't that prevent them from influencing others to imitate them? Particularly, as a father, I found this to be a bit of a conundrum. Leaving aside the Bible's caution, there is, let's face it, something rather obnoxious about continually announcing to the world that we have done this or that good deed, imagining that we are impressing listeners with our generosity, our largesse, our innate goodness, etc. I admit to being quite put off when someone's story seems to be begging for appreciative oohs and ahs, if not outright applause. On the other hand, how will a child model behavior that is continually kept secret from him/her? I wanted to teach my daughter, as best I could, about the importance of putting others first. I didn't think it was necessary to tell her about every time I did; but should I never? Furthermore, mightn't I be neglectful of my parental duties by failing to provide examples to her of exactly the behavior I hoped she would adopt?

Certainly, the best way to teach a child is not with words, but through deeds. Children naturally model behaviors they actually see, much more than those they merely hear about. Yet, the very point of most Angel Corps acts is that they are spontaneous. They arise unexpectedly, in the course of our daily activities. They come through our declaration, every morning, that we are 'in'. It is one thing - and a very good thing - to introduce our children to charitable activities by taking them along with us. When children participate with one or both of their parents in volunteer activities, they can experience for themselves the rewards to the self that such activities provide. But, as 'angels', much of our work is ad hoc, arising spontaneously in response to the numerous needs of our fellow beings. We don't plan them as outings, precisely because we don't plan them at all.

I eventually decided that there are times when it is appropriate to tell others about angel work, beginning with my daughter. My decision to write this book is an iteration of that earlier decision to let her know what I was up to. I believe that the Angel Corps is news worth spreading. It's good for each of us as individuals, and it's good for the planet. Looking back, it's a bit comical how much I experienced that ol' Catholic guilt when I first started telling my daughter about my rescues of worms, sharing food with stray cats, sharing food or money with homeless people, etc. What, after all, was there to feel guilty about? It's not like I expected to raise myself in her estimation with such reports. NO daughter thinks better of her father when he gushingly announces to her that he saved seven worms that day! I neither wanted nor expected that. I simply wanted her to be aware that some people, including her dad, engaged in such acts, so that she herself might eventually consider doing so as well. There was no pressure. I didn't throw a lot of 'shoulds' at her. I just wanted to plant the idea in her head that putting others first was an option, and allow that seed to flourish or wither according to her own judgment.

So, gradually, hesitantly, I decided to stretch out beyond the limitations of my early training. For one thing, the notion that "we already have our reward"; is that so bad? In this day and age, are any of us being kind to others primarily in hopes that 'somebody up there' is tallying up our acts and building up a storehouse for us? The true reward of being an 'angel' is the positive feelings our acts of kindness and generosity generate in the moments of performing them. Each time 'lil ol' us' is able to turn a frown upside down, or lift a burden from a troubled mind or a set of shoulders, the 'reward' is right there for the taking. Each such act strengthens our connection to something much larger than ourselves; a sort of Bank of Helpfulness that people have been depositing into and withdrawing from since the days of our earliest ancestors. Such a large, and too often untapped, store!

Here, not heaven, is where each small act makes a difference. If you or I do something charitable, and tell no one, that is still one lovely act. But maybe, just maybe, by telling others about it, we inspire them to behave similarly, and our act has now multiplied. And this world needs all the angel activity it can get!

Angels, NOT Doormats

In referring to putting others first as a 'necessity' (for our own personal growth, and for the healing of the planet), I in no way mean to imply that we should put ourselves last. Being an angel doesn't mean being a doormat; it doesn't mean letting others push you around or manipulate you, and it doesn't mean playing the role of martyr. An angel feels good about his or her acts of service; far from resenting the ones we serve, we feel profoundly grateful to them for providing us with an opportunity to act as our best selves.

Such distinctions have become harder than they need to be. We are taught, either through societal sins of omission or commission, to be selfish. The advertising industry daily - hourly even - assaults us with messages of what we need to have in order to be 'whole'. Its aim is to have us be both self-absorbed and forever unfulfilled, in need of that next product or service to complete us. Sports and entertainment and the cult of celebrity have trained us to look upon success, and 'winning', as the highest human achievements.

And the news (which is almost invariably bad) teaches us to to fear calamity around every corner. It is a dizzying array of signals that have taught us that we're in it for ourselves, we're on our own, and we'll never be good enough.

One of the greatest things about the Angel Corps is that, as one commits to it, it blows those fantasies apart. It breaks those spells. By making personal gestures of service on a continual basis, we achieve a greater sense of deep connection to others - and to formerly hidden parts of ourselves - that serve to gradually dissolve the corrosive selfishness that our dysfunctional society has steeped us in.

This enables us to become the exact opposite of self-ish: we become self loving. We love ourselves as we observe our transformation into more considerate and caring people, and more alert and attentive to others. We love the expanded world we grow into inhabiting. A world filled with beautiful interactions that have not been manufactured by media, but through personal contacts. We have real 'strangers' to care more about than the strangers on television shows, even though our interactions with them might last no more than a few seconds. Consequently, our days become more valuable. Putting others first has the seemingly paradoxical effect of making it easier to enjoy spending life with that one person that we spend each and every single moment with: our own self.

As a result of joining The Angel Corps, the lines between self and other, between our own needs and the ones of those who are 'in need', become wonderfully blurred. Whereas self-chosen martyrdom, and allowing ourselves to be somebody's doormat, create a deepening sense of separation between ourselves and others - and whatever sense we may have of a Guiding Principle to this universe - Angel Corps operations forge deeper connections. Our souls, or, if you prefer, the center of our being, will not be fooled. It is aware of which activities nourish it, and which harm it. Deep down, we all recognize the human need to be on the receiving end of help sometimes, and the giving end at others. A person who manages to go through an entire life bereft of either experience - if indeed such were even possible - will have missed out on the greatest opportunities that life offers.

Thus, Angel Corps activity can be seen as far more than the sum of myriad acts of service. Rather, it should be seen as a necessary cultural spearhead; toward reconnection and healing. It invites us to challenge the very principles upon which our modern society is founded upon - and to find them wanting. "I'm in'" means embracing one's true human identity, and abandoning the false, demeaning costumes of 'consumer' (of resources) and 'competitor' (for the 'right' values, truths, opinions, etc). Surprise! You are a member of a family (that includes all living creatures). Your relationship to life is exactly that - a relationship.

Just as becoming more willing to provide help is a process that some people take to more naturally than others, others find it very difficult - if not downright personally repugnant - to receive help. Thus, there will be times when our offers of help are unwelcome, perhaps even met with hostility. We may catch somebody on a particularly bad day. On the other hand, we may approach the situation with a surfeit of eagerness, as I often have. I am thinking of a time not long ago when I tried to assist a blind person who was going around in circles in Yokohama station. I have helped many blind people in similar situations, and nearly always have found them to welcome the assistance. I am sure it is frustrating for them to lose valuable time in a crowded station, when just one angel is all that is required to reorient them.

Since we must rely on their other senses to get their attention, I have found that a soft tap on the shoulder is usually accepted as a form of first contact. And afterwards, gently taking an arm to guide them. But, the person in Yokohama Station instantly resisted my initial touch. I felt his body tense up. "I don't need you", he curtly told me. I recognized that I wasn't entitled to any other response. It was I who had infringed on his space, and so he had a right to respond any way he chose. Still, I kept an eye on him, because he had clearly lost his bearings and was just moving between two walls. I approached him again. This time he was a little more receptive to being helped. But it turned out he had come way too far along the line he had ridden, and missed by several kilometers the station where he wished to make his connection to another line. Thus, I needed a bit of time to think, in order to orient myself and give him proper directions. He became frustrated, and just waved me off. He seemed determined to make it clear to me that he had no use for me.

I have no idea why he behaved this way. Perhaps he had experienced numerous frustrations with people who wanted to help him merely to feel good about themselves (was that what I was doing?, I wondered). Perhaps he had lost his sight only recently and was still in a great deal of anger, or perhaps denial, regarding his new circumstances. Perhaps his dismissal of me was his way of being defiant, not against a well-meaning stranger, but against a cruel fate that had robbed him of something invaluable. Whatever his reasons, they were his, and I had to remind myself that they really had nothing to do with me. I decided to honor his decision to reject my offer of help in such a forceful manner. His behavior stung, but I wasn't going to let it ruin my day. And I wasn't going to let it sour me on the idea of being an angel, not for one second. I took our exchange as a valuable lesson, and privately thanked him for it.

1% Inspiration, 99% Desperation

Sometimes an angel's work can take a form completely unexpected. From the moment we 'enlist', we connect to a vaster 'data store' than we personally possess. That sometimes enables us to intuit the most effective course of helpful action, even as it initially may appear counterintuitive. The result might even be that we receive deeper insight into the very nature of human insecurities.

Many years ago, my daughter Mika was new to the world, while I was similarly new to The Angel Corps. We were two beginners, in other words. As is typical in Japanese households with infants, Mika still slept in the same room with her mother and me, and had grown accustomed to the security our presence provided. One day, my wife returned home with the news that she would have to leave Tokyo for a few days on a business trip. We were both concerned about how Mika would handle that. Particularly the nights; how would she react to her first experience of separation from a parent?

The three of us went together to the train station on the evening of my wife's departure. On the platform, I held Mika up to the train window with one arm, and she and I waved goodbye as we watched her mother, also waving, disappear as the train pulled away. So far, so good. I brought a still cheerful Mika home, and the two of us had dinner. Still, nothing amiss. The evening wore on without event, and I put her to bed. I lay beside her while she gradually drifted off to sleep as smoothly and peacefully as any other night.

Congratulating myself for having done my part to raise such a well-adjusted baby, and grateful for her equanimous disposition, I gradually nodded off myself for what I hoped would be a long, uninterrupted period of peaceful sleep. And then, around two a.m., everything changed. I woke up to Mika's screaming out with lung power I never imagined she possessed. She was in a state of complete and utter panic. She frantically bawled, "Mama!"

What I had earlier feared was now coming to pass. The shock of waking up in the middle of the night, perhaps turning over to look at her mother - and then not finding her there - confronted her with a situation she simply couldn't process. All she could do was scream 'Mama!', over and over. And over. I grabbed her, and pressed her to my body tightly enough to dissolve every molecule of distance between us. I stroked her hair, and assured - and reassured - her that everything was okay, that mama was fine, and would soon return. I didn't expect her to understand every word, but I hoped that at least the tone of my voice would help to dispel her anxiety.

But, no dice. If anything, the intensity of her panic increased. I was dealing with, or rather failing to deal with, an infant in the throes of a full-on panic attack that showed no signs of abating any time soon. My 'help' wasn't helping at all, and even seemed to be making things worse.

What was I doing wrong? And did I have any other options than to just ride it out? I felt lost, and utterly lacking in the parental skills I had prided myself on just a few hours earlier. I gave up, and silently informed the Corps that I was open to suggestions. Suddenly, almost instantly, an odd notion popped into my head, "do what she does". As irrational, and downright bizarre as it seemed, I suddenly felt inspired to mimic Mika's own behavior. To do what she did.

Nothing else was working. My 'rational' approach had yielded no positive results. What did I have to lose? Feeling ridiculous, and hoping I could trust in the thickness of my apartment's walls to at least keep it a private matter, I began screaming at the top of MY lungs. I parroted Mika, matching her "Mama! for "Mama!"

Her first reaction, not surprisingly, was shock. At the very least, it was a dumbstruck shock, and I relished even that brief interlude of silence. She studied my face with a combination of disbelief and fascination. When she soon started screaming again, I resumed matching her. Her voice gradually became calmer (as did mine). Her body relaxed; I could feel it melt into my chest. Two minutes later, she was fast asleep, and slept peacefully through the remainder of the night. The panic didn't return when she woke up in the morning and mom was still gone. The problem had gone away.

What just happened? I asked myself. I tried to make sense of the unusual scenario that had just unfolded. And then, it hit me. By parroting Mika's screams, I was matching her emotionally. That caused her to feel less alone, more supported. She felt understood. Isn't that what we all want to feel?

Earlier, while trying to assure her that everything was okay, my actions had the opposite effect. To her, everything was NOT okay, and she was not about to be convinced otherwise. I was making her feel isolated in her experience; dismissing its validity. She became more inconsolable the more I went on that way.

What she really wanted, more than anything else, was validation. Her distress, her insecurity, her panic; she needed those to be understood and accepted by me. She wanted to know that we were in something together. As soon as she received that from me, she was able to move through her panic.

Now, the thing is, if I had been a trained child psychologist, I might have known immediately what to do, and grasped the theories behind it. But I was just a young dad, stumbling across the landmine-laden terrain of early stage parenthood. But, I had an ace in the hole. I had my membership in the Angel Corps. I got the help *I* needed in providing the help that *was* needed. Even more, I got a very valuable insight into human nature that has served me many times since, in a wide myriad of situations.

Words ARE Deeds

Each semester, in a university writing course I teach, I assign my students to write, and present in class, an essay related to the word 'appeal'. They are free to write anything they want, so long as it proceeds from consideration of that word. For example, they might try to dissect just what makes a popular movie series or musical act so appealing; what causes it to stand above the crowd? Alternately, if they are feeling confident, they can write about what they consider to be most appealing about themselves, perhaps using remarks they commonly hear from friends, lovers, etc., as evidence. Japanese (the majority of my students) are generally reluctant to discuss themselves in such a confident manner, which is one of the reasons I give the assignment. I want to see which of them will take the bait, and perhaps discover that occasionally honking ones' own horn can sound just the right note.

Recently, a student began his presentation with a heartbreaking story from his childhood. An incident caused him to wonder if he had any sort of appeal at all. One day, in his elementary school, he overheard one of his teachers whisper to another teacher, about him, 'just seeing him bums me out'. Can you imagine the pain those words inflicted? Those six words gave him a complex; that even without saying or doing anything, he simply had an aura that repelled others. He finished his speech a bit more hopefully, as his essay went on to detail ways in which he has managed to keep that awful thought at bay, and to feel at least okay about himself.

As soon as he finished, I knew that an angel task was before me. I couldn't just give him a perfunctory, 'nicely done, thank you' type evaluation. I told him that, I suspect, many people in this world have that same exact feeling about themselves. I told him that I knew it all too well, and have wondered that same thing ('maybe it's just...me') at times in my past. My voice cracked a little as I told him, 'But, it isn't true. It isn't true about you, or anyone else who fears that it might be true about them. There IS no such 'aura' of unlikability. It does not exist. It is tragic that you were ever made to feel that it might." Addressing the whole class, I said that my main reason for structuring the very course they were taking as I did was to teach them the power of words. His brief essay did more than the rest of the course combined in elucidating their dark side. I think I caught my student holding back a tear or two, although there was no need. There wasn't a person in the room who wouldn't have allowed him those, and more.

Words can mean so much, and therefore do so much. They are actions, in and of themselves. That teacher's cruel words hurt my student, likely far more than any physical pain he has ever experienced. They pummeled him like a bully's fists. Likewise, my words to him in the classroom had power. Certainly not enough to undo the damage that was done to him so long ago, but at least enough to support his own heroic struggle to stand tall in the face of it. As he said goodbye to me on his way out the classroom that day, I could see from the smile he beamed at me that he'd been given a boost.

Words, either spoken or selectively unspoken, become more important to us when we decide to serve in the Corps. The choice to offer encouragement, or the choice to withhold criticism, can - like all angel activities - do more for another person than we can ever know. Consider the powerful role words played in some of the stories I related earlier, such as the power of the words, "everything will be okay" to embolden, on that burning hill in Oakland. And the power of each wailed "Mama!" to comfort an infant, on a futon in Tokyo a year or so later.

The two most important words to me, as a member of the Angel Corps, are "I'm in". They are to me what 'Semper fi' is to a Marine. With them, I affirm my commitment to put others first, each day. I say them each morning, soon after rising, and again as I head out the door to encounter the world. Their influence on me has been profound.

Although none of us wants to be thought of as 'all talk, no action', there are times when the best - or only - service we can offer will be our words (as was the case that day in my writing class). How important, therefore, to choose them carefully. Our words, like our hands, our eyes, our backs and knees, our brains and our brawn, can - when placed in the service of the Angel Corps - become powerful tools of healing. They can even save lives. Let us, therefore, be generous with words that encourage. Let us make it a goal that our words have the effect of creating smiles. Alternately, when deep down we know that the thing we most want to say will rain on a parade, pick at an old wound, or possibly crush a soul, let us strive to perform what is often the hardest angel task of all; zip it.

Angels Everywhere!

When you live in a very large city, as I do, and particularly one as connected by public transportation as Tokyo, it is not difficult to find opportunities to be someone's angel. Anywhere between half to two thirds of my angel activities are performed in or around train stations. But that needn't discourage anyone from joining the Corps if one happens to live in more isolated circumstances (and compared to Tokyo, nearly any other circumstance counts as 'isolated'). Your commitment to the Angel Corps means the Angel Corps is committed to *you*. Your 'I'm in" will generate a response from the Corps, and acts of service will follow.

To confirm this, I asked a friend of mine who is living in a small town in Colorado, after having spent many years in Tokyo. He 'signed up' for the Corps only recently, and is surely one of its most enthusiastic new members. He writes, "here, everyone basically lives in their cars; there's not millions and millions of people on the streets like there are in Tokyo. So you can't run into situations here like you can over there."

Yet, he hastens to assure me that there are numerous opportunities to serve. He started by telling me about his friendly, supportive interactions with staff at restaurants and fast food joints, and the warm, appreciative smiles they generated. Such interactions must not be minimized, but rather seen as core Angel Corps operations. When one works long hours for low pay, the attitude of the customers one faces has a huge impact on how one sees oneself. People who are unconscious of this, and engage in the three B's of bad customer behavior (bullying, blaming and bossing around) do a lot of psychological damage, and a friendly angel or two can turn a checkout line into a lifeline.

My friend then went on to describe 'wasting' several minutes of his own time in a Costco, helping a fellow shopper locate a Costco-sized canister of pitted dates. Taking his commitment very seriously, he is also, voluntarily, helping a very talented - but not tech-savvy - woman he met through the internet create her business website. Himself a copywriter, he reports, "she didn't have a clue how to present herself on the Internet. I have been writing all her copy for her for free, basically making it possible for her to present herself on the web."

Finally, he says that he has written a flyer, at no charge, for a woman who is attempting to start her own housecleaning business. He adds, "she couldn't believe I would do such a thing, but as a member of the Angel Corps it is my duty."

All of this in less than three months since moving back to the States, and joining the Angel Corps shortly thereafter. As his words make clear, putting others first has now become an important commitment. He has created an exceptionally positive self image that he cultivates through his numerous choices to serve. Approaching seventy, he is now happier in his life than he has ever been. There is an infectious quality about the Angel Corps. It can rapidly become one of the most important things in your life. Imagine feeling as excited about your next chance to help somebody as you are about your next party, concert, sports event, golf outing, television episode, etc. Imagine putting others first as a 'hobby' that broadens your horizons while opening your heart, and it will become that for you, no matter where you live. It is truly for everyone.

Conclusion: So, Are You In?

I urge you to consider joining the Angel Corps. You can start right now, by silently confirming, 'I'm in' (and again tomorrow, and the next day, and so on). Or, if all that I've written has elicited little more from you than a feeling of, "well, duh ...", then: thank you for already being a member. To those who have been a member for many years - or many decades – allow me to doubly thank you, for helping me join. Each person's membership strengthens the Corps, which makes it easier for others to find out about it, and want to join. You have all, in a sense, helped me write this very book. And my hope is that by writing it, the Corps can add new members, and grow stronger still.

Anyone on the fence need not fear that they will instantly be flooded with requests requiring them to perform arduous tasks of service. Relatives won't suddenly appear, asking to borrow large sums of money that your reckless 'I'm in' has now obligated you to lend out. Neither should you fear that joining the Corps will cause you to flood your own mind with guilty thoughts that harangue you for not tithing, not becoming a vegan, etc, etc. The Corps doesn't operate like that.

What will happen is that you will start making better use of the numerous opportunities to serve that your life places in front of you simply through living. To be sure, there are people in this world who dedicate nearly their whole lives to putting others first; via volunteer activities that take them to disaster-stricken areas all over the globe, waking up two hours early every day in order to spend an hour handing out food at the local shelter, and so on. These angels may be seen and honored as the superstars of our beloved Corps. The higher ranks. But, you don't need to be like them. If such is your calling, you will surely find your way to it, eventually. Let me state quite plainly that I am not such a person. Although I've grown enough into my wings that I feel confident in affirming that I render at least one act of meaningful service each and every day, I haven't gradually morphed into a Schweitzer, and doubt that I ever will.

Since I therefore consider myself little more than a private in the Corps, do I lack the credentials to write a book about it? I think perhaps the opposite is true. I hope that the small, spur-of-the-moment acts of service that are my daily repertoire, and require so little of me in proportion to what they provide, will convince readers how very easy, but nonetheless beneficial, it is to join.

What I would love to see is for the simple, doable task of putting others first on a daily basis become a habit (as it has for me) as easily adhered to as buying one's coffee at a particular store, following a particular sport, or watching a particular news program. None of those activities require superhuman skill or effort, and neither does the Angel Corps. Thus, nothing about joining need be in the least intimidating. No massive makeover is required. One simply commits to going about one's life with a willingness to serve. The transformational power of sincerely offered humble acts of service is perhaps the greatest 'secret' in the human realm.

Perhaps one of the things that holds many of us back is a certain pridefulness. Being a 'servant' suggests being in a lower position. But it shouldn't. Service is the noblest of all actions. Service need not draw an unflattering contrast with 'master', but rather a favorable association with 'mastery'. Service is one of the surest avenues toward self mastery, as every Corps member can attest. Conversely, there are those who react negatively toward the idea of needing help. "I pulled myself up by my own bootstraps, and so can anyone else! Nobody helped me get where I am today!", they proudly proclaim. But....nobody? Not parents, teachers, friends, etc. etc.? Of course, all of us have benefitted from help sometimes. When looking back on the times when I needed help the most, some of which I have described in this book, their significance draws not from my own weakness, but rather from the incredible strength of the angels who were there for me. They inspire me! Without their acts of service, I wouldn't have learned to help others in need. If one has never benefitted from the help of another, how can one know how to be of help? And if one can't be of help, ever, to anyone, truly, what can one contribute to society? Therefore, let's honor and elevate the vital role a helping hand plays in our society, instead of making it into something shameful we would prefer not to admit to needing, and seen as only for the 'weak'.

I believe that greater awareness of the Angel Corps can help to grease the wheels for the one-eighty our society needs to make in order to get back on track, perhaps even to survive at all. In the final analysis, I don't know if the Angel Corps has the power to save the world, but I do know it has the power to make the world worth saving. In putting others first, I believe we will discover that our collective road leads upward.

With widened eyes, may I perceive
my fellow creatures' needs;
with willing legs and open arms
may I perform my deeds;
With smiles and healing as my goal, may I,
each day, go forth
And, putting others first, may I be shown
my life's true worth;
May many heed the call, and in so doing
evermore,
be strengthened by the knowing that
they're in the Angel Corps!

About the Author

Andrew Boerger is a writer, poet, artist and instructor living in Tokyo, Japan. Over the course of nearly two decades he has written (with co-author Kazuo Nagao) more than thirty books related to English instruction. He has illustrated for magazines, ad campaigns and children's books, and has produced several works of verse and prose, accompanied by his illustrations. With Hugh Ashton, he created 'the world's cutest detective', Sherlock Ferret, based on his furry chum, Vinnie.

His writing and artwork can be viewed on his blog at http://andysart-andyboerger.blogspot.jp

www.ingramcontent.com/pod-product-compliance
Lightning Source LLC
Chambersburg PA
CBHW071409080526
44587CB00017B/3224